LIVING DHARMA

A Guide to Daily Practice of Won Buddhism

LIVING DHARMA

A Guide to Daily Practice of Won Buddhism

Chung Ohun Lee, Ph.D.

Won World Publishing
New York

LIVING DHARMA:
A Guide to Daily Practice of Won Buddhism
April 2012

Library of Congress Cataloging-in-Publishing Data
ISBN 978-0-9855478-0-6

Won World Publishing
431 East 57th Street
New York, NY 10022
www.wonbuddhist.org

Printed in the United States

To those who aspire to transform and
to live an enlightened life for the benefit of all.

Acknowledgements

There are many people who supported the evolutions of this book as an essential tool for joyful everyday practice.

I am grateful to Patricia DelGiorno, Melody Johnson, Mary Coyle, Cliff Wallshein and Elizabeth Williams for their assistance in proofreading. Michael Dickes and Cherise Wolas have provided valuable clarifications from a newcomer's perspective. I am indebted to Doyeon Park who has encouraged me to produce this revised edition and worked hard to put materials together and for the design of this book. My deepest appreciation goes to Laura Samuels, the editor of Won World Publishing who provided precious suggestions.

My special thanks to the members of Won Buddhism of Manhattan who provided me with unconditional love and support, especially those who used the first edition of *Dharma Record* and offered me their encouraging comments.

May this book bring inspiration and joyful effort for everyday practice of Dharma. May this book bring self-empowerment, happiness and liberation.

Contents

Acknowledgements ix

Introduction 1

Beginning the New Path 3

Meditation 4

Patience 6

Enthusiastic Perseverance 7

Non-Attachment 8

Dharma Name 9

Daily Practice Guideline 11

Morning Practice Schedule 12

Evening Practice Schedule 13

Chanting Meditation 15

Sitting Meditation 16

Walking Meditation 19

Bowing Meditation 20

Koan Meditation 22

Affirmation Prayer 24

Loving-Kindness Prayer 25

Home Meditation Altar 26

Chants 29

Na-Mu Ah-Mi-Ta Bul 31

Essential Dharma of Daily Practice.................................... *32*

Il-Won-Sang Vow *33*

Heart Sutra.. *34*

Four Great Vows... *36*

The Precepts.. **37**

How to Follow Your Buddha Nature............................. **41**

Keeping a Dharma Record **43**

Why Keep a Dharma Record?....................................... *43*

How to Keep a Dharma Record? *44*

Dharma Record **47**

Weekly Dharma Record.. *48*

Keeping a Spiritual Journal **75**

Epilogue.. **77**

About the Author... *78*

Endnotes/Glossary... *81*

Introduction

The objective of this book is to help you to establish everyday practice with joy. It will guide you to build the power of cultivating good habits. It will assist you in creating consistent daily practice of meditation and mindfulness; to transform yourself; and to become enlightened - not only for your own benefit, but also for the benefit of all.

Meditation brings serenity, awareness, gratitude and meaning into our trivial daily activities. Building a consistent practice of meditation is essential if you are to experience these positive qualities in your mind and body.

In the modern world, we need to update our thinking to meet the challenges of the 21st century. With the rapid advancement of material civilization and its ever-expanding new technology, we need to cultivate spirituality in equal measure.

Living Dharma is based on my personal experience of teaching Won Buddhism for more than three decades in the United States. Over the years, I have reinterpreted the essentials of Won Buddhist teachings for the English-speaking population without losing the true meaning of the original teaching. These teachings have been well received around the world and at the United Nations.

This volume emphasizes the simplicity and relevance of daily Dharma practice for contemporary Western society.

Living Dharma is a practical guide to help you cultivate spiritual awareness and to remove negativity from your life.

Living Dharma is a simple, yet effective, system to gain self-discipline. With self-discipline and consistent practice, you will achieve your goals and live a peaceful and joyful life.

If you already have a deep commitment to practice meditation daily, *Living Dharma* will make it easier to be consistent. The easy to follow program helps you track what to do and what not to do.

Consistency is the key to creating a space in your life for daily Dharma practice. By faithfully following the simple guidelines of this book on a daily basis, you will experience inner peace and joy, wisdom, happiness and loving-kindness. Keep *Living Dharma* near you and make it a priority in your daily life. Begin a new life today.

Beginning the New Path

When I search for my True Self,
I begin the new path of awakening.
When I cultivate my spirituality,
I enjoy living my life with deep gratitude.

When I awaken to the truth:
I find beauty and goodness in myself.
I find beauty and goodness in others.
I find beauty and goodness in everything.

When I awaken to the truth,
I AM CREATING MYSELF!

I begin a new life every day.
I begin a new way of being on earth,
with new ways of thinking and
new ways of dealing with external challenges.

I examine my habits carefully
and investigate my attitudes and intentions.
With this inward journey,
I become one with my Larger-Self which connects with the
whole world.

My spiritual journey continues with deep questions:
Who am I?
Where am I?
Why am I?

Meditation

Meditation is the art of calming my mind.
Meditation is an inward journey toward liberation.
Meditation means serenity and calmness in life.
Meditation helps me to calm distracted and restless minds
and uncovers my own Buddha Nature within.

Following my breath and sustaining awareness
through the entire inhalation and exhalation,
I achieve focus, composure, tranquility, clarity, equanimity,
illumination and Samadhi concentration.

Meditation is a self-healing process.
Meditation is a cleansing time to let go of all distractions.
Meditation is a sacred technique to understand
my emotional and psychological state.

Meditation is a blessed practice of living in the moment.
Mediation embodies the here and now
with what is happening
in my mind, in my body, in my experience,
and in the world around me.

Meditation practice is the sacred investment in myself.
Meditation makes me happier and content.
My happiness comes from meditation, resilience,
equanimity, inner peace and joy.

Meditation is a nurturing and self-empowering activity.
The more I practice meditation,
the greater benefit I experience.
During meditation I directly experience the bliss, Nirvana,
wisdom and compassion of my own Buddha Nature.

Meditation wakes me up
from ordinary consciousness into a state in which
each moment becomes a peak experience.
Meditation becomes a part of my everyday activity.

Every day is a beginning of a new life,
full of awe and wonder and
filled with infinite gratitude.

When I meditate,
I breathe together with the whole universe.
When I meditate,
I become one with the universe.
When I meditate,
I *am* the universe.

Patience

Patience is the strength of mind and heart.
Patience comes from seeing the whole picture, and
Understanding the universal principle:
What goes around comes around.

Patience is the antidote to anger.
Patience enables me to face the challenges and difficulties
of life, without losing inner peace and stability.

I cultivate inner strength and serenity.
I stay calm and compassionate
in the face of aggression and misunderstanding.

Patience requires a change in my attitude about life.
I accept the twists and turns in life graciously.
I endure the ups and downs of life gracefully.
I shift my consciousness to see the goodness in others,
to see the beauty and truth in everything.

The most sacred patience is the time
I give myself for my understanding of
The Dharma and Buddhist teachings:
Buddha Nature in everything and
Buddha Nature everywhere.

Enthusiastic Perseverance

In the practice of meditation and spiritual journey,
I establish joyous effort and
enthusiastic perseverance in daily life.

To eliminate dissatisfaction, suffering, unhappiness,
depression, stress, negativity and shortcomings,
I build steady and consistent practice of meditation.
Meditation is the source of my infinite happiness.

When I am consistent in practice of meditation and Dharma
in spite of difficulties, obstacles or discouragement
I enjoy uplifting energy, vigor, vitality, strength,
perseverance, diligence and enthusiasm.

Perseverance is the key to my success
for everyday practice with joy.
I value continuous and persistent effort.
I enjoy and appreciate my consistent practice.
I honor and treasure my regular sitting.

Non-Attachment

Any attachment to past words, deeds or thoughts
hinders what I do in the present moment.
I spoil the new life of every moment
and weaken the present by viewing it through
the color of the lens of the past or future.

Through mindfulness and self-discipline,
I let go of my attachment to everything,
simplify my needs and wants
and start a new life every day.

If my heart-mind flows like a river,
not living in the past,
not living in the future,
I live here and now in this moment.

Life is a process.
Life is a continuous becoming.
Life is transient.

Every moment is a new life.
Every moment is a new beginning.
Every moment is a peak experience.

Dharma Name

Upon entering the Won Buddhist path,
you begin your spiritual journey
with a new Dharma name.

This name represents
Your spiritual rebirth.
As you live and seek
enlightenment and liberation,
not only for your own benefit,
but for the benefit of all living beings.

A Dharma name signifies the beginning of a
new journey of spiritual practice to awaken
to the Dharma. Receiving a Dharma name is
an acknowledgment of one's connection to
the practice on the path of awakening.

Daily Practice Guideline

Set your mind and vow to begin daily meditation practice. If you live with your family or roommates, let them know about your meditation practice so you may have their support as well.

Choose a space in your home that is the most comfortable and quiet, and create a home meditation altar there. You can have a meditation cushion, Il-Won-Sang[1], meditation bell, candle, incense, or anything that inspires your dharma practice. Reduce any clutter and create a peaceful atmosphere which is free of distractions.

Find a regular time to practice every day. It can be 20 to 30 minutes, or more each day. You may first try mediating for one week. After a week, you may consider expanding it to a month, then to 100 days, then a year or even a lifetime. Morning practice can help you prepare your day with a new fresh mind; while evening practice can give you time to reflect on your day and to relax. You choose morning and/or evening practice. It doesn't matter what time of day you practice. What is important is that you *develop consistency*. **Begin Today!**

Morning Practice Schedule

1. Prayer

2. Sitting Meditation

3. Koan Meditation

4. Chant of the Il-Won-Sang Vow

5. Chant of the Heart Sutra[2]

6. Review the Essential Dharma of Daily Practice

Evening Practice Schedule

1. Chanting: Na-Mu Ah-Mi-Ta-Bul

2. Sitting Meditation

3. Reading of Spiritual Teachings

4. Review of the Essential Dharma of Daily Practice

5. Keeping a Dharma Record and Spiritual Journal

6. Prayer

Chanting Meditation

Chanting meditation is a method of practice that focuses the mind when it is distracted among a myriad of active thoughts. Chanting creates a one-pointed mind by reciting a simple phrase, or Sutra. It's about letting go of all your wandering thoughts, worries and stress by reciting the words. When chanting, you must concentrate your mind on your own voice and the sound of chanting itself.

1. Straighten your back, neck and head and center your body. Do not swing or shake your body.

2. Keep your chanting voice level to a volume appropriate to your energy.

3. To get hold of the mind, keep a rhythm with a Mok-Tak (wooden gong) or you can use meditation beads.

4. Concentrate on your own voice of chanting itself.

5. Let go of each and every thought and maintain a relaxed mind.

6. Chanting constantly reflects on the original state of your Buddha Nature.

7. In this way, you become united with the sound of your own voice and begin to awaken to the Buddha within.

Sitting Meditation

1. Sit comfortably in a crossed-legged position, straighten your back, neck and head. Align your ears with your shoulders. Keep your nose in line with your navel and center your body.

2. Rest your hands on your lower thighs. Your chin slightly tucked in.

3. Close your eyes or open them halfway with your gaze resting on the floor about two or three feet in front of you.

4. Center all your focus and concentration on your Dahn Jon: the Dahn Jon is about three fingers below your navel, inward two inches, in the center of your lower abdomen.

5. Take a deep breath in, down to the Dahn Jon area. Then, expanding your lower abdomen, breathe out, contracting. Be aware of your belly rising and falling. Let your mind watch and observe your breathing in and out.

6. Gently close your mouth. Make sure your jaw is relaxed and touch the tip of your tongue to the roof of your mouth just behind your front teeth.

7. When you meditate well, lots of pure saliva will gather in your mouth, you may swallow it quietly.

8. If you have pain in your leg or back, you may quietly switch your position. If you have distractions, be aware of them and gently let them go by returning to your breath.

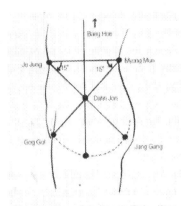

The location of the lower Dahn Jon

 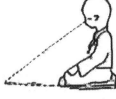 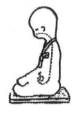

Those who have made a great vow to the great Way should not hope to accomplish it quickly. With quick steps one cannot walk a long distance; with an impatient mind one cannot achieve the great Way. That tall tree is the result of a small shoot growing for many years; Buddhas and bodhisattvas are the result of accumulating merits over a long period of time."

Sotaesan

Walking Meditation

Walking Meditation, as a form of meditation in action, is essentially about the awareness of movement as we note the component parts of the steps. In walking meditation we use the experience of walking as our *focus*. As we walk, we become mindful of our walking movement and try to keep our awareness of the experience of walking as the basis of developing greater awareness. With this practice, we can easily apply meditation into our daily activity. The great thing about walking meditation is that we can do it anytime we are walking even it's just walking from home to the subway and from the subway to the office, even in the noise and bustle of a big city.

Walking meditation is a wonderful way of transforming something we do every day into practice for our awakening.

"Walking meditation is really to enjoy the walking – walking not in order to arrive, but just to walk. The purpose is to be in the present moment and aware of our breathing and our walking, to enjoy each step. Therefore, we have to shake off all worries and anxieties, not thinking of the future, not thinking of the past, just enjoying the present moment." - Thich Nhat Hanh

Bowing Meditation

For thousands of years, Buddhist cultures have used bowing meditation as part of their spiritual and physical practices. Bowing meditation is practiced both as a preparation for sitting meditation and as a form of meditation. Bowing meditation is **not used as a form of worship.** We do not bow down to anything exterior. But we bow in humble acceptance and respect to our own inner Buddha Nature.

In bowing, we totally pay respect to the all-pervading virtue of wisdom, which is the buddha within ourselves. In making the bow, we should move neither hastily nor sluggishly but simply maintain a reverent mind and humble attitude. When we bow too fast, the bow is then too casual a thing; it might even indicate we are hurrying to get it over and done with. This is frequently the result of a lack of reverence.

The Standing Bow

This bow is used upon entering the dharma room, and in greeting one another and our teachers. The body is erect, with the weight distributed evenly and the feet parallel to each other. Palms are placed together with straightened, closed fingers pointing upward. As the bow is made, the body bends at the waist, so that the torso forms an angle with the legs of approximately 45 degrees. The hands do not move relative to the face, but remain in position and move only with the whole body.

The Deep Bow (Full Prostration)

This bow is more formal than the standing bow and requires a continuous concentration during its performance so that it is not sloppily done.

The bow itself begins in the same way as the standing bow, but once the body is bent slightly from the waist, the knees bend and one assumes a kneeling position. From the kneeling position, the movement of the torso continues, with the hands separating and moving into a position parallel with the forehead. As the bowing movement progresses, the backs of the hands come to rest just above the floor and the forehead is lowered until it rests upon the floor between the hands. The person bowing then gets to his feet once again in a smooth motion.

In kneeling, actually the knees do not touch the ground simultaneously, but in sequence: first, the right and then the left knee touches the ground. The same is true for the right and left hands and right and left elbows, in that sequence. In practice, however, the interval between right and left sides touching the ground may be so minute as to be unnoticeable. In bowing, movement should not be jerky or disjointed, but should flow smoothly and continuously without either disruption or arrested motion.

Koan Meditation

Koan meditation is a method to directly see your Buddha Nature by asking a spiritual question. Koan means a transcendent question in Zen tradition and it is used as means of gaining spiritual awakening. Koan generally contains aspects that are inaccessible through rational understanding, yet accessible to intuition.

Essential Cases for Questioning

1. What is the sound of one hand clapping?
2. "Mind is Buddha." What does this mean?
3. "All things are created by the mind." What does this mean?
4. What body did you have before your parents conceived you?
5. When a person is in deep, dreamless sleep, where is the numinous awareness that makes one sentient?
6. Why is it that there is Samsara for sentient beings but liberation for all the Buddhas?
7. "A person who practices well is not separated from the Buddha Nature." What is this practice which is not separated from the Buddha Nature?
8. How are mind, nature, principle and energy the same?
9. Are all things in the universe subject to arising and ceasing or free from arising and ceasing?

10. The karmic retributions of *cause* and *effect* among all things in the present life occur by knowing one another. But how do the retributions of later lives occur, when they have forgotten their past lives and no longer recognize one another?

11. "Heaven and Earth know without knowing anything." What does this mean?

12. The numinous awareness of people who attain Nirvana is merged with the Dharmakaya. How, then, do individual spirits become divided again and the standard for distinguishing past and future lives come into existence?

13. "I have a volume of scripture that is written without paper or ink. It does not contain a single word, yet always radiates light." What does this mean?

Affirmation Prayer

Dharmakaya Buddha,

May I renew my commitment to cultivate my spirituality.
May I restore my inner peace and joy in order to build
peace on Earth.

May I let go of everything to live a new life
to start a new day each day.

I pray everyone may become emboldened in heart,
filled with compassion and wisdom and find the path that
leads to love and peace.

May I spend more time in meditation and silence
to understand myself completely.

May I nurture myself to uncover my Buddha Nature, to
uncover my inborn wisdom to see the truth: the truth about
myself, the truth about others, and the truth about the
universe.

May this practice of Dharma deepen and strengthen my
love and wisdom for all.

Loving-Kindness Prayer

May I be happy.

May I be healthy.

May I be safe.

May I be content.

May I love myself just as I am.

May you be happy.

May you be healthy.

May you be safe.

May you be content.

May you love yourself just as you are.

Home Meditation Altar

We live in a city that demands 100% of our attention. All day long we live with stress because of our jobs or families. When we create a home altar, we create the environment to motivate us to practice more often. Being able to wake up in the morning and start your day, meditating will help you strengthen your mind for whatever you will encounter that day. Lighting a candle and incense at night, while you meditate, will calm your spirit and help you to relax before going to bed. You can meditate at any time of day by yourself or with your family. Meditation is the way to reach the path toward inner serenity and awakening. So put together an altar in your home today.

*"Won Buddhist items are available at the temple
for the making of your altar."*

- Il-Won-Sang: The symbol of Won Buddhism.

- Gong: The striking of the gong is to calm your mind in making the transition from the outer world to the inner world. We ring the gong 10 times to connect with the cosmic energy in the universe.

- Mok-Tak: Made of cedar wood perfect for chanting.

- Incense Holder: This beautiful white incense holder holds up to three incenses at a time. It protects your altar from any incense falling on your table, keeping it always looking clean.

- Incense: We carry three different kinds of incense all with wonderful fragrances.

Chants

When chanting, concentrate your mind on your own voice
and the sound of chanting itself.

Na-Mu Ah-Mi-Ta Bul

Return to Amita[3] Buddha, the Buddha of infinite light
and life that is within all of us.

Essential Dharma[4] of Daily Practice

1. Let us maintain the concentration of our Buddha Nature[5] so that we may be free from disturbance at all times and in all places.

2. Let us maintain the wisdom of our Buddha Nature so that we may be free from delusion at all times and in all places.

3. Let us maintain the compassion of our Buddha Nature so that we may be free from negativity at all times and in all places.

4. Let us replace disbelief, greed, laziness, and delusion with faith, courage, perseverance, and an inquiring mind.

5. Let us change resentment into gratitude.

6. Let us cultivate confidence and self-reliance.

7. Let us change resistance to learning into willingness to learn.

8. Let us change resistance to teaching into willingness to teach.

9. Let us overcome selfishness in order to serve the universal good.

Il-Won-Sang Vow

Il-Won[6] is the realm of Sa-ma-dhi[7] be-yond all words and speech; the gate-way of birth and death, tran-scen-ding being and non-being; the o-ri-gin of u-ni-verse, pa-rents, li-ving be-ings and laws; the o-ri-gi-nal na-ture of all bud-dhas[8], bo-ddhi-sat-vas[9], hu-mans and sen-tient be-ings.

Il-Won mani-fests both as per-ma-nence and im-per-ma-nence.
Viewed as per-ma-nence, *Il-Won* ex-ists through-out et-er-ni-ty and un-folds in-to an in-fi-nite world.
Viewed as im-per-ma-nence, *Il-Won* un-folds in-to in-fi-nite worlds through the cy-cle of for-ma-tion, du-ra-tion, de-cay and void of the u-ni-verse; and the birth, a-ging, ill-ness, and death of all things; through the way we use our minds and bo-dies in the four forms of birth,[10]
we trans-form through the six realms of ex-ist-ence,[11] pro-gres-sing or re-gres-sing with grace a-ri-sing from harm, or harm from grace.

By mo-del-ing our-selves af-ter *Il-Won-Sang*, the Dhar-ma-ka-ya[12] Bud-dha, we vow to prac-tice with ut-most de-vo-tion, to cul-ti-vate our minds and bo-dies per-fect-ly;
to know life and u-ni-ver-sal princi-ples per-fect-ly;
to use our minds and bo-dies per-fect-ly;
thus pro-gres-sing ra-ther than re-gres-sing
and re-cei-ving grace ra-ther than harm,
un-til we at-tain the great pow-er of *Il-Won*,
and be-come one with the na-ture of *Il-Won*.

33

Heart Sutra

A-va-lo-ki-te-sva-ra[13] *Bo-dhi-satt-va,* when prac-ti-cing deep *Praj-na*[14]*Pa-ra-mi-ta*[15] saw that all five *skan-dhas*[16] are emp-ty and be-came free from all suf-fering and dis-tress.

Sha-ri-pu-tra[17], Form does not dif-fer from emp-ti-ness, emp-ti-ness does not dif-fer from form. Form is emp-ti-ness, emp-ti-ness is form. The same is true of sen-sa-tions, per-cep-tions, im-pul-ses, con-scious-ness.

Sha-ri-pu-tra, All dhar-mas are emp-ty; they do not ap-pear or dis-ap-pear, are not taint-ed or pure, do not in-crease or de-crease. There-fore in emp-ti-ness, no form, no sen-sa-tion, no per-cep-tion, no im-pulse, no con-scious-ness. No eyes, no ears, no nose, no tongue, no bo-dy, no mind; no sight, no sound, no smell, no taste, no touch, no ob-ject of mind; no realm of eye, ear, nose, tongue, bo-dy, and mind con-scious-ness.

No ig-nor-ance, nor ex-tinc-tion of it, no old age and death, nor ex-tinc-tion of them. No suf-fering, no cause of suf-fering, no ces-sa-tion of suf-fering, no path; no wis-dom, no at-tain-ment with no-thing to at-tain.

The Bo-dhi-satt-va re-lies on *Praj-na Pa-ra-mi-ta,* and the mind is no hin-drance; with-out an-y hin-drance, no fears ex-ist; free from de-lu-sion, one dwells in *Nir-va-na*[18].

All Bud-dhas of the past, pre-sent, and fu-ture re-ly on *Praj-na Pa-ra-mi-ta* and at-tain su-preme en-ligh-ten-ment.[19]

There-fore, know that *Praj-na Pa-ra-mi-ta* is the great tran-scend-ent man-tra[20], is the great en-ligh-tening man-tra, is the ut-most man-tra, is the in-com-para-ble man-tra, which is a-ble to end all suf-fering. This is true, not false. So pro-claim the *Praj-na Pa-ra-mi-ta* man-tra, which says,

Gone_, gone_, gone be-yond_, far be-yond_, now a-wa-kened.

Ga-te! Ga-te! Pa-ra ga-te! Para-sam ga-te! Bo-dhi! Sva-ha[21]! (**3 times**)

Four Great Vows

Sentient beings are numberless; we vow to save them.
Delusions are endless; we vow to eliminate them.
Teachings are infinite; we vow to learn them.
Supreme Enlightenment is inconceivable; we vow to attain
it.

The Precepts

From the Buddhist perspective, all of the moral precepts are rules of training, not commandments. We undertake them as a way of directing our heart, out of care for the world and ourselves, rather than as an externally imposed set of laws.

The importance of moral disciplines was emphasized by the Buddha himself. When he was passing away, the Buddha was asked who would succeed him, and he said that the practice of morality should be the guide, therefore naming *moral discipline* as his successor.

In Won Buddhism, there are thirty precepts. At first, we introduce ten precepts for beginners. After these are mastered, we take the next set of ten precepts for unswerving faith. After we master them, we move to the final set of ten precepts.

The Ten Precepts for Beginners in Faith

1. Do not kill without due cause.

2. Do not steal.

3. Do not commit sexual misconduct.

4. Do not consume intoxicants without due cause.

5. Do not gamble.

6. Do not use harsh speech.

7. Do not quarrel without due cause.

8. Do not embezzle public funds.

9. Do not borrow or lend money between close friends without due cause.

10. Do not smoke tobacco.

Ten Precepts for the Unswerving Faith

1. Do not make decisions about public affairs by yourself.

2. Do not speak about the faults of others.

3. Do not be obsessed by the pursuit of gold, silver, and precious gems.

4. Do not be obsessed with wearing clothes.

5. Do not make friends with the immoral people.

6. Do not talk while someone else is talking.

7. Do not be untrustworthy.

8. Do not use flattery to seek approval.

9. Do not sleep at an improper time without due cause.

10. Do not join in immoral and improper pleasures.

Ten Precepts for the Struggle Between Dharma and Mara[22]

1. Do not be arrogant.

2. Do not have more than one spouse.

3. Do not eat the flesh of four-legged animals without due cause.

4. Do not be lazy.

5. Do not be deceptive.

6. Do not speak disrespectfully.

7. Do not be jealous.

8. Do not be greedy.

9. Do not be angry.

10. Do not have delusion.

How to Follow Your Buddha Nature

1. Believe not just in the person alone, but in the Dharma.

2. Ponder the Dharmas taught by various persons and believe in the very best of them.

3. Having been born as humans among all the four types of birth, we should have a love of learning.

4. A knowledgeable person should not neglect new learning just because he or she has knowledge.

5. Do not indulge in wine and dalliance, but use the time to inquire into Truth.

6. Do not cling to your biases.

7. When responding to any matter, maintain a respectful state of mind and fear the rise of covetous greed.

8. Teach yourself day by day, hour by hour.

9. When something goes wrong, do not blame others, but examine yourself.

10. If you learn of another's fault, do not reveal it but use it instead to perceive your own faults.

11. If you learn of another's achievements, proclaim them to the world and never forget them.

12. So long as they are doing what is right, try to understand the palpable reality of others' situations by thinking of your own case.

13. Even at the risk of your life, always do what is right, despite how much you may dislike doing it.

14. Even at the risk of your life, never do what is wrong, no matter how much you may want to do it.

15. Do not exhort others to do anything they do not wish to do, but be concerned only with your own affairs.

16. If you form a wish and want to see it fulfilled, compare everything you see and hear to that wish and study its fulfillment.

Keeping a Dharma Record

The power of cultivating good habits begins with a Dharma Record. Keeping a Dharma Record will help you to establish everyday practice with joyful effort.

When you are aware of your own thoughts, words and actions, you can mindfully choose constructive thoughts, words and actions.

Why Keep a Dharma Record?

When you become aware of your actions, words and thought in each and every moment, you can choose a good habit over a bad one. Before you can change your bad habits, you must *identify* and *keep track* of them. By faithfully keeping a Dharma Record, you will become aware of your actions, not only at the end of the day, but also at every moment. Gradually, each good action and each small awakening will open your heart to the Buddha within. Eventually, small awakenings of everyday life will lead you to supreme enlightenment.

How to Keep a Dharma Record?

Throughout the day, you can keep track of your practice. Whenever you make a mindful choice to practice meditation and the Dharma, you can keep a Dharma Record at the moment as well as at the end of the day.

1. Meditation and Wisdom

❖ **Prayer**: Put a √ if you prayed in the morning and evening. If you did not, put a dash mark.

❖ **Meditation**: Put a √ if you meditated in the morning, in the evening or during the day. If you did not, put a dash mark.

❖ **Chanting**: Put a √ if you practiced chanting meditation. If you did not, put a dash mark.

❖ **Reading Spiritual Teachings and Scripture**: Put a √ if you studied the scriptures and read spiritual teachings. If you did not, put a dash mark.

2. Precepts

From the thirty precepts or Dharma, select ones relevant to you and write them in the spaces on the chart. Add your own precepts such as exercise, healthy eating or organize.

If you observed, put a √. If you have violated a precept, put a dash mark or record the number of the incidents.

On the last day of each week, after completing your Dharma Record, add up the number of checks and dashes. When you observe your actions every day, you will begin to experience small awakenings. You should not be discouraged at first, if you have more dashes (—) than checks (√) on your record. In the beginning this is to be expected.

3. Mindfulness

The Dharma of good habits begins with mindfulness and awareness. In order to examine whether you have done something mindfully, you record the number of times you have, or have not, acted with mindfulness. When you carefully decide on what to do and what not to do, then you are being mindful of your actions. When you have not acted mindfully, then you have been unmindful in your actions.

There is a space for you to record mindfulness and unmindful actions. Keep track of specific areas in which you wish to be more mindful. These selections are at your discretion.

Choose aspects of your life that you wish to improve. For example, perhaps you wish to get to work on time, or to live here and now, in the moment. Simply write in the spaces provided: "here and now" or "on time." Then keep track according to the aforementioned directions how often you were mindful and unmindful, or successful and unsuccessful with each task. Total your score at the end of each day. For the best results, observe your progress over time.

In the beginning, the standard by which you determine which actions were performed mindfully is not related to whether the results of those actions were good or bad; but whether they were selected mindfully and carefully.

When your study matures, however, then the standard becomes whether the results of the actions were good or bad, and successful or unsuccessful.

Now begin your Dharma Record today, and keep it every day with motivation and joyful practice.

Dharma Record

Weekly Dharma Record

Month: Year:

Content \ Date		Sun	Mon	Tue	Wed	Thu	Fri	Sat	Total √	Total —
Meditation & Wisdom	Prayer									
	Meditation									
	Chanting									
	Reading									
Precepts										
	Mindful									
	Unmindful									

Weekly Dharma Record

Month: Year:

Content \ Date		Sun	Mon	Tue	Wed	Thu	Fri	Sat	Total √	Total —
Meditation & Wisdom	Prayer									
	Meditation									
	Chanting									
	Reading									
Precepts										
	Mindful									
	Unmindful									

Weekly Dharma Record

Month: Year:

Content \ Date	Sun	Mon	Tue	Wed	Thu	Fri	Sat	Total √	Total —
Meditation & Wisdom — Prayer									
Meditation									
Chanting									
Reading									
Precepts									
Mindful									
Unmindful									

Weekly Dharma Record

Month:　　　　Year:

Content \ Date	Sun	Mon	Tue	Wed	Thu	Fri	Sat	Total √	Total —
Meditation & Wisdom Prayer									
Meditation									
Chanting									
Reading									
Precepts									
Mindful									
Unmindful									

Weekly Dharma Record

Month: Year:

Date / Content	Sun	Mon	Tue	Wed	Thu	Fri	Sat	Total √	Total —
Meditation & Wisdom — Prayer									
Meditation									
Chanting									
Reading									
Precepts									
Mindful									
Unmindful									

Weekly Dharma Record

Month:　　　　　Year:

Content \ Date	Sun	Mon	Tue	Wed	Thu	Fri	Sat	Total √	Total —
Meditation & Wisdom — Prayer									
Meditation									
Chanting									
Reading									
Precepts									
Mindful									
Unmindful									

Weekly Dharma Record

Month: Year:

Content \ Date	Sun	Mon	Tue	Wed	Thu	Fri	Sat	Total √	Total —
Meditation & Wisdom — Prayer									
Meditation									
Chanting									
Reading									
Precepts									
Mindful									
Unmindful									

Weekly Dharma Record

Month:　　　　　Year:

Content \ Date	Sun	Mon	Tue	Wed	Thu	Fri	Sat	Total √	Total —
Meditation & Wisdom — Prayer									
Meditation									
Chanting									
Reading									
Precepts									
Mindful									
Unmindful									

Weekly Dharma Record

Month:　　　　　Year:

Content ╲ Date	Sun	Mon	Tue	Wed	Thu	Fri	Sat	Total √	Total —
Meditation & Wisdom Prayer									
Meditation									
Chanting									
Reading									
Precepts									
Mindful									
Unmindful									

Weekly Dharma Record

Month: Year:

Content \ Date	Sun	Mon	Tue	Wed	Thu	Fri	Sat	Total √	Total —
Meditation & Wisdom Prayer									
Meditation									
Chanting									
Reading									
Precepts									
Mindful									
Unmindful									

Weekly Dharma Record

Month: Year:

Date / Content	Sun	Mon	Tue	Wed	Thu	Fri	Sat	Total √	Total —
Meditation & Wisdom — Prayer									
Meditation									
Chanting									
Reading									
Precepts									
Mindful									
Unmindful									

Weekly Dharma Record

Month: Year:

Content \ Date	Sun	Mon	Tue	Wed	Thu	Fri	Sat	Total √	Total —
Meditation & Wisdom — Prayer									
Meditation									
Chanting									
Reading									
Precepts									
Mindful									
Unmindful									

Weekly Dharma Record

Month: Year:

Date / Content	Sun	Mon	Tue	Wed	Thu	Fri	Sat	Total √	Total —
Meditation & Wisdom — Prayer									
Meditation									
Chanting									
Reading									
Precepts									
Mindful									
Unmindful									

Weekly Dharma Record

Month:　　　　Year:

Content \ Date		Sun	Mon	Tue	Wed	Thu	Fri	Sat	Total	
									√	—
Meditation & Wisdom	Prayer									
	Meditation									
	Chanting									
	Reading									
Precepts										
	Mindful									
	Unmindful									

61

Weekly Dharma Record

Month: _____ Year: _____

Content ╲ Date	Sun	Mon	Tue	Wed	Thu	Fri	Sat	Total √	Total —
Meditation & Wisdom Prayer									
Meditation									
Chanting									
Reading									
Precepts									
Mindful									
Unmindful									

Weekly Dharma Record

Month:　　　　　Year:

Content ╲ Date		Sun	Mon	Tue	Wed	Thu	Fri	Sat	Total	
									√	—
Meditation & Wisdom	Prayer									
	Meditation									
	Chanting									
	Reading									
Precepts										
	Mindful									
	Unmindful									

Weekly Dharma Record

Month:　　　　Year:

Content \ Date	Sun	Mon	Tue	Wed	Thu	Fri	Sat	Total √	Total —
Meditation & Wisdom Prayer									
Meditation									
Chanting									
Reading									
Precepts									
Mindful									
Unmindful									

Weekly Dharma Record

Month: Year:

Content \ Date	Sun	Mon	Tue	Wed	Thu	Fri	Sat	Total √	Total —
Meditation & Wisdom — Prayer									
Meditation									
Chanting									
Reading									
Precepts									
Mindful									
Unmindful									

Weekly Dharma Record

Month: Year:

Content \ Date	Sun	Mon	Tue	Wed	Thu	Fri	Sat	Total √	Total —
Meditation & Wisdom — Prayer									
Meditation									
Chanting									
Reading									
Precepts									
Mindful									
Unmindful									

Weekly Dharma Record

Month: _____ Year: _____

Content \ Date	Sun	Mon	Tue	Wed	Thu	Fri	Sat	Total √	Total —
Meditation & Wisdom — Prayer									
Meditation									
Chanting									
Reading									
Precepts									
Mindful									
Unmindful									

Weekly Dharma Record

Month: Year:

Content \ Date	Sun	Mon	Tue	Wed	Thu	Fri	Sat	Total √	Total —
Meditation & Wisdom Prayer									
Meditation									
Chanting									
Reading									
Precepts									
Mindful									
Unmindful									

Weekly Dharma Record

Month: Year:

Content \ Date		Sun	Mon	Tue	Wed	Thu	Fri	Sat	Total √	—
Meditation & Wisdom	Prayer									
	Meditation									
	Chanting									
	Reading									
Precepts										
	Mindful									
	Unmindful									

Weekly Dharma Record

Month: Year:

Content \\ Date	Sun	Mon	Tue	Wed	Thu	Fri	Sat	Total √	Total —
Meditation & Wisdom — Prayer									
Meditation									
Chanting									
Reading									
Precepts									
Mindful									
Unmindful									

Weekly Dharma Record

Month: Year:

Content \ Date	Sun	Mon	Tue	Wed	Thu	Fri	Sat	Total √	Total —
Meditation & Wisdom Prayer									
Meditation									
Chanting									
Reading									
Precepts									
Mindful									
Unmindful									

Weekly Dharma Record

Month: Year:

Content \ Date	Sun	Mon	Tue	Wed	Thu	Fri	Sat	Total √	Total —
Meditation & Wisdom Prayer									
Meditation									
Chanting									
Reading									
Precepts									
Mindful									
Unmindful									

Weekly Dharma Record

Month: Year:

Content \ Date	Sun	Mon	Tue	Wed	Thu	Fri	Sat	Total √	Total —
Meditation & Wisdom Prayer									
Meditation									
Chanting									
Reading									
Precepts									
Mindful									
Unmindful									

Weekly Dharma Record

Month: Year:

Content \\ Date	Sun	Mon	Tue	Wed	Thu	Fri	Sat	Total √	Total —
Meditation & Wisdom Prayer									
Meditation									
Chanting									
Reading									
Precepts									
Mindful									
Unmindful									

Keeping a Spiritual Journal

In addition to your Dharma Record, you can keep a Spiritual Journal about your awakenings and impressions. It is meditative writing for self-examination and spiritual understanding and expression of daily life. It will help you to assess your progress in understanding the Dharma, universal principles and your own Buddha Nature.

You can keep a Spiritual Journal about how you use your mind and body each day so that you gain ability to make mindful choices in action, whatever you do. For example, if you get into trouble, you can examine why you got into trouble, what caused it and how you can handle the same situation better in the future. And you can journal about what you need to do in order to not repeat the same mistake. You include your thoughts, self-reflections and perception of your daily life. You can record important new insights.

A Spiritual Journal should be a meaningful and rewarding experience. It is your journey into self-knowledge and awareness.

A Spiritual Journal helps you to understand your past and navigate your own future. It allows you to be real with yourself and assist you in self-discovery.

Epilogue

I hope that you have found *Living Dharma* useful to establish your good habits of Dharma practice. Your spiritual practices are the key to developing your spiritual life and uncovering your own Buddha Nature.

The importance of *Living Dharma* is to deepen and strengthen your practice of meditation and Dharma with your consistent everyday practice. It is your time to nurture your own Buddha Nature and pay attention to what you are feeling.

I am confident that, as you practice with *Living Dharma*, you will create the appropriate daily arrangements capable of practicing meditation and cultivating your innate goodness and inborn wisdom.

In your practice of meditation and spiritual journey, it is good to establish joyous effort and enthusiastic perseverance in your daily life. *Living Dharma* should be practiced with joyful perseverance which is the enlightened quality of energy, vigor, vitality, strength, diligence, enthusiasm, continuous and persistent effort.

I hope that the ideas and instructions of *Living Dharma* contribute to your progress, happiness and joy.

About the Author

Ven. Dr. Chung Ohun Lee is the Founding Head Minister and guiding Spiritual Teacher of Won Buddhism of Manhattan (WBM). She established WBM in 1993 in order to teach Buddha Dharma to the English-speaking population. Ven. Lee shares her expertise in the Dharma, Buddhist meditation, the basic teachings of Buddhism as well as Won Buddhist philosophy and practice with the Sangha.

Chung Ohun Lee is a recognized international leader in interreligious dialogue and cooperation. She has represented Won Buddhism at the United Nations (UN) since 1992. She has held several important UN committee positions:

- Founding Co-Chair of *Values Caucus* at the UN (1994-1995)

- President of *Committee of Religious NGOs* at the UN (1995-1997)

- Chair of *Universal Ethics Millennium Conference* at the UN (2000)

- Chair of *World Culture Open Conference* at the UN (2004)

- Chair of *International Conference on Creative Economy* in Rwanda (2006)

- Convener of the conference on *Advancing Cooperation between the United Nations and World's Religions* at the UN (2008)

- Chair of the *G20 Universal Ethics Conference, G20 Women Leaders' Summit, G20 Dialogue among Civilizations, Cultures and Religions and G20 International Interfaith Retreat* in South Korea (2010)

In these capacities, Dr. Lee presented Won Buddhist philosophy and spirituality to international audience.

Ven. Lee is a long-time advocate of inter-religious understanding and cooperation and is the Co-President of Religions for Peace, the largest international interfaith organization, a position she has held since 1999.

Ven. Lee is the author of *Vision for a New Civilization: Spiritual and Ethical Values in the New Millennium* (2000*)* and *Dharma Record: New Mind and New Body* (1994).

Ven. Lee began practicing Won Buddhism in 1971 and received full ordination in Won Buddhism in 1981, in South Korea. After her ordination Ven. Lee taught Buddha Dharma in Flushing, New York for twelve years. She holds Ph.D. in Religious Education from New York University.

Her focus is Won Buddhist spirituality, the practical application of Buddha Dharma in the contemporary world, the role of religion in our time and engaging Won Buddhist perspectives in global issues.

Endnotes/Glossary

[1] **Il-won-sang**: The visual symbol of Il-Won or One Circle. Il-Won-Sang, which represents the ultimate Truth is the object of faith and the model of practice in Won Buddhism.

[2] **Sutra**: A scriptural narrative, especially a text traditionally regarded as a discourse of the Buddha or one of his disciples; literally "thread."

[3] **Amita**: Sanskrit word which literally means "boundless light and boundless life". Amita Buddha is the presiding Buddha of the Western Paradise, or Pure Land, in which all beings enjoy boundless happiness. The Western Paradise of Ultimate Bliss is not to be understood as a location but as a state of consciousness.

[4] **Dharma**: Sanskrit word. Central notion of Buddhism and used in various meanings. 1) The cosmic law, the "great norm" underlying our world; above all, the law of karmically determined rebirth. 2) The teaching of the Buddha, who recognized and formulated this "law"; thus the teaching that expressed the universal truth. 3) Norms of behavior and ethical rules. In the plural, dharmas refer to all things, visible or invisible (that is, phenomena)

[5] **Buddha Nature**: According to the Mahayana view, the true, immutable and eternal nature of all beings. Since all beings possess buddha nature, it is possible for them to attain enlightenment and become a buddha, an enlightened one.

[6] **Il-won**: Korean word. It literally means One Circle. It refers to Dharmakaya Buddha, which is the original source of all things in the universe, and the original nature of all sentient beings. This represents the fundamental Truth, which is the basis of all religion.

81

[7] **Samadhi:** Sanskrit word which literally means "establish, make firm"; collectedness of the mind on a single object through calming of mental activity. Samadhi is a non-dualistic state of consciousness in which the consciousness of the experiencing "subject" becomes one with the experienced "object"- thus, is only experiential content. This state of consciousness is often referred to as "one-pointedness of mind"; this expression, however, is misleading on one point on which the mind is "directed." However, samadhi is neither a straining concentration on one point, nor is the mind directed from here (subject) to there (object), which would be a dualistic mode of experience.

[8] **Buddha:** Sanskrit word, which literally means "awakened one." 1) A person who has achieved the enlightenment that leads to release from the cycle of existence and has thereby attained complete liberation. 2) The Buddha of Siddartha, historical Buddha, who was the founder of Buddhism.

[9] **Bodhisattva**: Sanskrit word meaning "enlightened being". In Mahayana Buddhism a bodhisattva is a being who seeks buddhahood through the systematic practice of the perfect virtues (paramita) but renounces complete entry into Nirvana until all beings are saved.

[10] **Four forms of birth**: Viviparous, as with mammalia; oviparous, as with birds; moisture or water born, as with worms and fishes; metamorphic, as with moths from chrysalis, or with devas, or in hells, or the first beings in a newly evolved world.

[11] **Six realms of existence:** Six ways or destinies of sentient beings: Hells, hungry ghosts, animals, malevolent nature spirits, human existence and deva, or Heavenly existence. Sentient beings experience a succession of rebirths. Until liberation, a

being is imprisoned in samsaric realms which are conditioned by greed, anger and delusion. In Won Buddhism, it is understood as psychological states of human beings.

[12] **Dharmakaya**: Sanskrit word meaning the Dharma Body, the Cosmic Body, or the Essential Body of the Buddha. The true nature of the Buddha, which is identical with transcendental reality, the essence of the universe. The Dharmakaya is the unity of the Buddha with everything existing. At the same time it represents the "law"(Dharma), the teaching expounded by the Buddha.

[13] **Avalokitesvara**: Means one of the most important Bodhisattvas of the Mahayana. The literal meaning of Avalokitesvara is variously interpreted: two interpretations are "Lord Who Looks Down" and "He/She who Hears the Sound (Outcries) of the World." Avalokitesvara embodies one of the two fundamental aspects of buddhahood, compassion and wisdom.

[14] **Prajna**: Refers to an immediately experienced intuitive wisdom; its meaning cannot be conveyed by concepts or in intellectual terms.

[15] **Paramita**: Literally "that which has reached the other shore," the transcendental. The paramitas, generally translated as "perfections," are the virtues perfected by a bodhisattva in the course of his/her development.

[16] **Skandha**: Term for the five aggregates, which constitute the entirety of what is generally known as "personality." They are form, sensation, perception, mental formation and consciousness. The characteristics of skandhas are birth, old age, death, duration and change. They are regarded as without essence, impermanent, empty and ridden of suffering.

[17] **Shariputra:** One of the most eminent and revered disciples of the Buddha. The Heart Sutra is written in the form of a dialogue between Shariputra and the Bodhisattva of Great Compassion.

[18] **Nirvana:** The realization of the true nature of the mind, identical with the true nature of human beings - the Buddha Nature.

[19] **Anuttara-Samyaksmbodhi:** Literally, "perfect universal enlightenment." It is the full form of samyaksarnbodhi (enlightenment of a complete buddha).

[20] **Mantra:** A power-laden syllable or series of syllables that manifests certain cosmic forces and aspects of the Buddha.

[21] **Gate, gate, paragate, parasamgate, bodhi svaha:** The mantra uttered by the Bodhisattva; translates literally as, " Gone, gone, gone beyond, far beyond, now awakened."

[22] **Mara:** literally means murder, destruction. Mara personifies unwholesome impulses, unskillfulness, the "death" of the spiritual life. He is a tempter, distracting humans from practicing the spiritual life by making the mundane alluring or the negative seem positive.